RETORTS

LEN TOMAKA

ILLUSTRATIONS BY ROLLIN MCGRAIL

Gotham Books

30 N Gould St.
Ste. 20820, Sheridan, WY 82801
https://gothambooksinc.com/

Phone: 1 (307) 464-7800

© 2025 *Len Tomaka*. All rights reserved.

No part of this book may be reproduced, stored in a retrieval system, or transmitted by any means without the written permission of the author.

Published by Gotham Books (March 18, 2025)

ISBN: 979-8-3484-9429-2 (H)
ISBN: 979-8-3484-9427-8 (P)
ISBN: 979-8-3484-9428-5 (E)

Because of the dynamic nature of the Internet, any web addresses or links contained in this book may have changed since publication and may no longer be valid.

The views expressed in this work are solely those of the author and do not necessarily reflect the views of the publisher, and the publisher hereby disclaims any responsibility for them.

PREFACE

I have always admired people who have a quick wit (including those otherwise known as smart alecks) and who use wisecracks or sarcasm in their retorts. Quick-witted people seem to take pride in responding with some type of comment when they hear someone's statement.

Over the years, I have compiled a list of the better comebacks that I have heard every day in the real world. The list grew and grew, and, by golly, I realized that these retorts contain many life lessons (as well as wisecracks) that can be helpful to anyone.

The key to this book is setting up the situations to which each retort is responding.

This book is my attempt to enable passive people to be more outgoing.

I suggest discussing these retorts at a family function or gathering of friends, as many of these situations will be familiar and lead to hilarious banter.

I hope you find it interesting and amusing.

Len

TABLE OF CONTENTS

PREFACE iii
CHAPTER 1 1
Reality 1
CHAPTER 2 45
Reassurance 45
CHAPTER 3 59
Caution 59
CHAPTER 4 91
Encouragement 91
CHAPTER 5 105
Zingers (Retorts with Zest) 105
ACKNOWLEDGEMENTS 141
ABOUT THE AUTHOR 142

CHAPTER 1
Reality

When a friend doesn't realize he or she is in a bad situation:

"AND HOW IS THAT WORKING OUT FOR YOU?"

When a friend is getting involved with something that you think he or she is not capable of handling well:

"YEA, WELL GOOD LUCK WITH THAT."

As an aid to get to the conclusion or a prefix to a final thought:

"WELL AT THE END OF THE DAY."

or

"THE BOTTOM LINE IS THIS."

or

"YOU DO THE MATH."

When a friend is having trouble finding a replacement for someone he or she has lost:

"YOU CAN'T REPLACE GOLD WITH SILVER."

When someone who did not accept your offer before has come back to take you up on it:

"THAT SHIP HAS SAILED."

or

"THAT TRAIN HAS LEFT THE STATION."

When a friend doubts your capability:
"REALLY."
or
"BEEN THERE DONE THAT."
or
"YEA LIKE YOU'RE SO SMART."

When someone reminds you that you are not playing by the rules:

"IT IS NOT WRITTEN IN STONE."

When a friend is reluctant to make a decision:

"BITE THE BULLET."

or

"THE DIE IS CAST."

or

"GET OFF YOUR DEAD BUTT."

When you hesitate to be truthful with someone because you are holding something back from them:

"LET ME BE HONEST WITH YOU."

When someone says, "Don't worry; I'll take care of it":

"PROMISE!"

When you admit that you made a mistake:
   "I LEAPED BEFORE I LOOKED."
   or
   "I WAS THINKING WITH MY MOUTH."

When you can't seem to put all the pieces together and something is nagging at you:

"THERE IS STILL SOMETHING IN THE BACK OF MY MIND."

When someone is being obstinate and won't accept your decision:

"LOOK - IT IS WHAT IT IS."

or

"IT DOESN'T WORK THAT WAY."

When something is discovered that was overlooked:

"IT GOT LOST IN THE SHUFFLE."

When a friend is bouncing around looking for a solution:

"AS A PRACTICAL MATTER."

When a situation requires a quick decision:

"IT'S A NON STARTER."

or

"IT'S A NO BRAINER."

To explain the pressure of what seemed to be a decision that was not well planned out:

"MY BACK WAS TO THE WALL."

or

"I DIDN'T HAVE A CHOICE."

If you are starting a meeting where you have many gray areas to be discussed:

"LETS AGREE TO DISAGREE."

or

"LET'S SEE IF WE CAN GET ON THE SAME PAGE."

or

"LET'S PEEL AWAY SOME LAYERS OF THE ONION."

If a successful friend is complaining about not getting enough cooperation:

"AH, IT MUST BE LONELY AT THE TOP."

When someone is prolonging an argument with you:

"OH, SO NOW WE HAVE TO GO TIT FOR TAT."

When a friend didn't put enough effort in and is complaining about the result:

"LIFE IS NOT A DRESS REHEARSAL."

When a person shows impatience listening to you:

"TO MAKE A LONG STORY SHORT."

To start off from a request for help (or apology) with a person of authority:

"I HUMBLY COME TO YOU WITH MY HAT IN MY HAND."

When someone is accusing you of trickery:
"WHAT YOU SEE IS WHAT YOU GET."

When someone is taking advantage of someone else:

"BE CAREFUL - WHAT GOES AROUND COMES AROUND."

To console someone who is suddenly overloaded with work:

"WHEN IT RAINS IT POURS."

When someone is feeling sorry for themselves forgetting the big picture:

"STOP AND SMELL THE ROSES."

or

"COUNT YOUR BLESSINGS."

When someone incorrectly thinks he or she is being treated unfairly:

"SUCH IS LIFE."

or

"THE FACT OF THE MATTER IS THIS."

When circumstances change due to timing:
"THAT WAS THEN - THIS IS NOW."

When someone underestimates you:
"MAKE NO MISTAKE."

When someone is expressing disappointment in getting older and starting to forget things:

"IT DOESN'T GET ANY BETTER."

or

"IT DOESN'T GET ANY EASIER."

When a well off person is hesitating about paying for a special purchase he or she would love to acquire:

"YOU CAN'T TAKE IT WITH YOU."

If someone offers a deal or to buy something that is too costly for you:

"TOO RICH FOR MY BLOOD."

When someone is dissatisfied with an inferior product:

"WELL YOU GET WHAT YOU PAY FOR."

When someone tries to make it up to you after taking advantage of you:

"NOW YOU ARE ADDING INSULT TO INJURY."

or

"TOO LITTLE TOO LATE."

or

"TWO CAN PLAY AT THAT GAME."

When you think friends are holding back their opinions:

"A PENNY FOR YOUR THOUGHTS."

If someone persists with a point that he or she says is important but that really doesn't matter:

"THAT IS NEITHER HERE NOR THERE."

To confirm to a friend that you understand what his or her point is:

"TELL ME ABOUT IT."

or

"YOU'RE TELLING ME."

When a person is complaining about another person who is always negative:

"CRYBABIES NEVER GROW UP."

When a friend is upset because a person he or she thought was close to him or her has been unavailable:

"LOYALTY WILL STOP FROM SOME PEOPLE WHEN THEIR NEED FOR YOU STOPS."

At a dinner party where someone complains about a certain dish:

"IT'S NOT WHAT YOU EAT BUT WITH WHOM YOU EAT."

CHAPTER 2
Reassurance

"You were a plow horse in a past life."

If a friend is lamenting a lost companion:

"DON'T BE SAD IT'S OVER, BE GLAD IT HAPPENED."

If a friend is complaining about a good but late result:

"BETTER LATE THAN NEVER."

When a friend wishes you good luck in a situation:

"FROM YOUR LIPS TO GOD'S EARS."

If a person isn't confident to take an action that you think he or she should:

"I WOULD DO THAT IN A HEARTBEAT."

When a friend is not happy with his or her progress:

"YOU HAVE TO CRAWL BEFORE YOU CAN WALK."

When a friend gets out of a bad situation:
"YOU ARE OFF THE HOOK."
or
"YOU DODGED A BULLET."

When a person is talking about taking revenge:
"LIVING WELL IS THE BEST REVENGE."

When a friend says he or she is undereducated and won't be considered for advancement:

"YOU ARE A DIAMOND IN THE ROUGH."

When someone appears to need reassurance:
"YOU CAN TAKE THAT TO THE BANK."

If a friend is in a quandary regarding different steps to take:

"DO THE RIGHT THING."

or

"TO THINE OWN SELF BE TRUE."

When you meet an old friend that you haven't seen in a while:

"YOU ARE A BREATH OF FRESH AIR."

When someone gives you a surprise treat:

"THAT'S JUST WHAT THE DOCTOR ORDERED."

CHAPTER 3
Caution

If a person deceived you or lied to you in the past:

"FOOL ME ONCE SHAME ON YOU -
FOOL ME TWICE SHAME ON ME."

When a person keeps trying to convince you of something that you don't accept:

"SAVE YOUR BREATH."

or

"LET'S BACK UP A LITTLE BIT."

When a friend is about to be looking to change his or her lifestyle:

"TROLL IN THE PROPER WATERS."

When you feel a friend is being starry-eyed upon entering a situation or deal and not seeing obvious obstacles:

"DON'T BITE OFF MORE THAN YOU CAN CHEW."

or

"IF YOU PLAY WITH FIRE YOU COULD GET BURNT."

or

"TREAD EASY."

or

"KEEP YOUR IMAGINATION SEPARATE FROM FACT."

or

"THERE IS ANOTHER SIDE TO THAT COIN."

or

"YOU'RE MISSING THE FOREST FOR THE TREES."

or

"THERE ARE TWO SIDES TO EVERY STORY."

or

"JUST LET IT GO."

If you are trying to express an overwhelming situation weighing on your mind:

"THERE IS A BLACK CLOUD HANGING OVER MY HEAD."

or

"THERE IS A HEAVY WEIGHT ON MY SHOULDERS."

If a friend gets angry describing a problem with someone:

"WHEN YOU SHOW YOUR ANGER YOU HELP YOUR OPPONENT."

If a friend is surprisingly troubled by a negative comment made by someone:

"CONSIDER THE SOURCE."

or

"DON'T BE THIN-SKINNED."

or

"DON'T LOOK BACK. THAT MAY STOP YOU FROM GOING FORWARD."

When a friend is excitedly jumping into a goal he or she has always dreamed of, but you feel that he or she did not consider all the possible ramifications that may be involved:

"BE CAREFUL WHAT YOU WISH FOR."

If a group of people are standing in a cluster instead of being in their work stations:

"ONE GRENADE GETS 'EM ALL."

When you feel a friend is unaware of the time restraints in a situation:

"THE CLOCK IS TICKING."

or

"DON'T PUT OFF UNTIL TOMORROW WHAT YOU CAN DO TODAY."

or

"YOU SNOOZE YOU LOSE."

or

"DON'T BEAT AROUND THE BUSH."

or

"DON'T LET THE GRASS GROW UNDER YOUR FEET."

When you notice that a friend spends lavishly on nonessential things but gets every drop out of the toothpaste tube:

"PENNY WISE AND POUND FOOLISH."

When someone is having trouble learning a competitive sport:

"IF YOU SET THE BAR TOO LOW, YOU WILL ALWAYS HIT YOUR MARK."

When you are in a meeting and nobody is bringing up an important item:

"THERE IS STILL THE MATTER OF THE 800 POUND GORILLA IN THE ROOM."

If you are in a debate and feel the other person isn't absorbing what you are saying:

"LET'S BACK UP A LITTLE BIT."

or

"MY POINT IS."

When a friend can't quit trying to get two people who don't like each other to get along:

"NEVER THE TWAIN SHALL MEET."

When a friend is asking your opinion on a matter about which you have little knowledge:

"WHILE THIS IS NOT MY CUP OF TEA - I THINK THIS."

When discussing a person who is not trustworthy:

"CONSIDER THE SOURCE."

or

"I WOULDN'T WANT THAT PERSON IN MY FOXHOLE."

or

"THAT PERSON IS A SNAKE IN THE GRASS."

or

"THAT PERSON IS A WOLF IN SHEEP'S CLOTHING."

or

"A LEOPARD CAN'T CHANGE ITS SPOTS."

or

"YOU CAN'T JUDGE A BOOK BY ITS COVER."

When a friend is complaining about being neglected by other friends:

"OUT OF SIGHT OUT OF MIND."

When you have learned that a friend is getting deeper in debt by overspending:

"IF YOU DON'T DIG THE HOLE, YOU DON'T HAVE TO DIG YOUR WAY OUT OF IT."

When someone says he or she has you over a barrel in a contest just before the end:

"OH YOU THINK SO, HUH?"

When a friend is critical of someone and is overreacting negatively about that person:

"LIVE AND LET LIVE."

or

"LET SLEEPING DOGS LIE."

or

"LOOK AT THE POT CALLING THE KETTLE BLACK."

or

"PEOPLE WHO LIVE IN GLASS HOUSES SHOULDN'T THROW STONES."

When a friend should be grateful to someone who is being generous but instead is indignant and feels he or she is entitled to more:

"DON'T BITE THE HAND THAT FEEDS YOU."

or

"BEGGARS CAN'T BE CHOOSERS."

or

"IF YOU CAN'T STAND THE HEAT GET OUT OF THE KITCHEN."

or

"YOU'RE ENTITLED TO NOTHING."

or

"YOU CAN'T HAVE YOUR CAKE AND EAT IT TOO."

or

"YOU CAN'T PUT THE GENIE BACK INTO THE BOTTLE."

or

"DON'T GET CAUGHT WITH YOUR HAND IN THE COOKIE JAR."

When a friend is thinking of overreacting in a vengeful way without realizing that he or she might be harming themselves at the same time:

"DON'T CUT OFF YOUR NOSE TO SPITE YOUR FACE."

When a friend is having a hard time deciding on purchasing something:

"DO YOU NEED IT OR DO YOU WANT IT?"

When you sense that someone isn't telling you all the facts:

"IS THERE ANYTHING ELSE YOU WOULD LIKE TO TELL ME?"

or

"DO YOU HAVE SOMETHING UP YOUR SLEEVE?"

When a person appears just after you were talking about him or her:

"SPEAK OF THE DEVIL!"

When you feel confronted by overwhelming odds in a negotiation:

"WHAT IS THIS - A STACKED DECK?"

When you need more time when someone is pressuring you for comment:

"WE'LL TALK."

CHAPTER 4

Encouragement

When a friend is going through a rough patch in his or her life:

"If YOU ARE GOING THRU HELL KEEP GOING."

or

"YOU ARE A DIAMOND IN THE ROUGH."

or

"IT IS ALWAYS DARKEST BEFORE THE DAWN."

When you see an old friend that you haven't seen in quite a while:

"WE ARE STILL HERE."

When a friend is tiring in an effort and wants to stop:

"KEEP GOING; THERE IS NO REST FOR THE WEARY."

or

"STAY THE COURSE."

If you feel someone is resting on his or her laurels and not being active enough:

"KEEP MOVING, IT IS HARDER TO HIT A MOVING TARGET."

or

"THE BEST DEFENSE IS A GOOD OFFENSE."

To encourage someone who is off to compete:
"GO GET 'EM TIGER!"

When a person is hesitating to take action:
"THE BALL IS IN YOUR COURT."
or
"BREAK A LEG,"
or
"WAKE UP!"
or
"DO SOMETHING - ANYTHING!"

When a friend is saying that a clothing style is too revealing:

"IF YOU GOT IT FLAUNT IT"

If a friend is not happy with petty items holding him or her up from completing a task:

"DON'T SWEAT THE SMALL STUFF."

When a friend is sharing that he or she is apprehensive regarding a decision that might be taken the wrong way:

"DON'T WORRY, YOU'RE ENTITLED."

If you feel a friend is being passive in the midst of a conflict:

"IT'S TIME TO TAKE OFF THE GLOVES."

or

"YOU HAVE TO NIP IT IN THE BUD."

or

"KEEP YOUR EYE ON THE PRIZE."

or

"TELL IT LIKE IT IS."

or

"ARE YOU KIDDING? THIS IS RIGHT UP YOUR ALLEY."

or

"THEY'RE TOO BUSY THINKING ABOUT THEMSELVES."

When a friend is overreacting to a problem:

"TREAT A DISASTER LIKE AN ANNOYANCE."

CHAPTER 5
Zingers (Retorts with Zest)

When a friend is leaving and saying "See you later":

"THANKS FOR THE WARNING!"

or

"NOT IF I SEE YOU FIRST!"

When you confirm to a friend a time you are to meet later:

"BE THERE OR BE SQUARE."

When someone stumbles but catches him- or herself from falling:

"HOW WAS YOUR TRIP?"

or

"SEE YOU NEXT FALL!"

When a friend says "Have a nice day":
"DON'T TELL ME WHAT TO DO."

When a friend tells you something that is unfortunate that has happened to him or her:

"YIKES!"

or

"I WOULD RATHER HAVE A ROOT CANAL."

When someone shows up for work earlier than normal:

"WHAT'S THE MATTER COULDN'T YOU SLEEP?"

When someone shows up late for a morning meeting:

"GOOD AFTERNOON!"

When a person apologizes for missing a couple of meetings:

"WERE YOU GONE?"

When someone asks you if you have seen someone:

"IT IS NOT MY TURN TO WATCH HIM."

After beating an opponent when you are both of equal skill:

"GEE, YOU PLAYED THE BEST THAT I HAVE EVER SEEN YOU PLAY."

or

"OH MY GOD, YOU LOOKED REALLY GOOD OUT THERE."

When a friend shows up and is crabby:

"WHAT'S THE MATTER, DID YOU GET UP ON THE WRONG SIDE OF THE BED THIS MORNING?"

When people are talking negatively about you just far enough away from you that they think you might not hear them:

"YOU KNOW ... I CAN HEAR YOU!"

When you are in a circle of friends and everyone is sharing his or her thoughts but no one is asking your opinion:

"WHAT AM I ... NOTHING?"

When a friend has underestimated someone who now is taking control from him or her:

"MY MY, HOW THE WORM HAS TURNED."

When a friend shows up with a bruised face:

"DID YOU THINK HE SAID STAND UP WHEN HE REALLY SAID SHUT UP?"

When you are caught wearing a style that you previously saw on a friend and that friend notices:

"JUST REMEMBER, IMITATION IS THE BEST FORM OF FLATTERY."

When a friend is complaining about a relationship that is beginning to go sour:

"AH, THE BLOOM IS OFF THE ROSE."

When someone doesn't notice you and steps in front of you and then says "I'm sorry" or "Excuse me":

"WHY, WHAT DID YOU DO?"

When someone is constantly being a jerk:

"YOU ARE A ONE WAY STREET - THE WRONG WAY."

When you are taking over for someone who can't seem to get a handle on a task:

"WATCH AND LEARN."

If you encounter a person on an intercepting path who is carrying something, give the person the right of way and say:

"YOU HAVE GOT THE LOAD."

If someone doubts that you are providing all the facts:

"THERE IS NOTHING UP MY SLEEVE."

or

"WHAT YOU SEE IS WHAT YOU GET."

If you get on the elevator and push a button that doesn't light up, say to another person on the elevator:

"MAYBE I'M DEAD."

When a subordinate keeps giving you useless suggestions, tell that person the Jesse James story:

> Jesse James was going down the aisle of the train he was robbing and missed an expensive broach that a woman was wearing. Another woman said, "Jesse, you missed that broach behind you."
>
> Jesse said, "WHO'S ROBBING THIS TRAIN, YOU OR ME?"

When you need to defuse a situation after telling someone something that may have turned out to be offensive:

"I'M JUST SAYING."

When a person tells you "I was born on third base":

"I WAS BORN ON THIRD BASE WITH A BIG LEAD OFF."

When something bad happens and you want to show confidence that you could leave:

"I'VE GOT A POCKETFUL OF MONEY AND A FULL TANK OF GAS."

When someone teases you because he or she has the upper hand:

"WHATEVER!"

When a showoff is raving about his or her knowledge of something:

"BOY DO I FEEL STUPID."

When your opponent makes a nice put away in your tennis match and a passerby yells out, "Nice shot":

"MIND YOUR OWN BUSINESS."

When someone rudely makes a point during a discussion to you and you feel angry:

"IT WAS NOT WHAT YOU SAID BUT HOW YOU SAID IT!"

When you want to have the final word as you walk away from a heated discussion and you are sure you have the upper hand and you just want to gloat, use the following; they have no specific meaning, but they sure are a lot of fun to say:

"AND THAT'S A FACT JACK!"

or

"END OF CONVERSATION."

or

"I REST MY CASE."

or

"AND YOU CAN TAKE THAT TO THE BANK." or

"TSK, TSK YOU LOSE."

or

"THAT'S THE WAY THE MOP FLOPS."

or

"THAT'S THE WAY THE COOKIE CRUMBLES."

or

SING like a child, "NA NA NA NA NA NAAA."

or

OR THE CLASSIC - JUST STICK YOUR TONGUE OUT AT THEM.

or

SILENCE THEM WITH A STARE AS YOU WALK AWAY.

ACKNOWLEDGEMENTS

My gratitude and thanks to Terry and Lanny Passaro, Mike DeVito, Bob Johnson, Ed Hoveke, Michael Koenigsknecht, Phillip Tomaka, Fr. Niles Gillen O. Carmel, and Jethro Hurt for their help and all the fun we had bantering about this book.

ABOUT THE AUTHOR

Len Tomaka is a native Chicagoan. His college is Washburne Trade School, where he completed a five-year Chicago Local Union #597 Pipe Fitter apprenticeship. He has worked at every level in the field—apprentice, pipe fitter, foreman, job site superintendent, and estimator and project manager for mechanical contractors in the heavy industrial and commercial industries. He finished his career with his consultancy to mechanical contractors. He spent five years in the United States Marine Corps Reserve and holds three US patents.

This is Len's second book. His first is Aphorisms, Adages, and Advice for the Children I Never Had.

www.ingramcontent.com/pod-product-compliance
Lightning Source LLC
LaVergne TN
LVHW012244070526
838201LV00090B/119